Green Blade

2015 Edition

The Magazine of the
Rural America Writers' Center
Plainview, Minnesota

Published through a special arrangement with

SHIPWRECKT BOOKS PUBLISHING COMPANY

IN®
DIE

Minnesota

Editorial Board
Nicole Borg
Carolyn Bizien
Dean Harrington
Nancy Hengeveld
Nicholas Ozment
Shipwreckt Books

Cover Painting
Melissa Lammers

Layout, Interior & Cover Design
Shipwreckt Books

Table of Contents

Editor's Note
Nicole Borg

It is the growing season here in Southeastern Minnesota. Many of us have finished planting our gardens—straight rows of carrots, tomatoes, onions, green beans. I cannot help but dream of a long, hot summer harvesting the vegetables I have labored over, but also the tasty offerings at the farmers markets, those things I am too impatient to grow myself—asparagus, corn, and broccoli.

At the Rural America Writers' Center, we are fortunate to have a year-round growing season, where we partake in the literary fruits of some of Minnesota's most talented writers. Monthly, we gather to sample from a buffet of regional talent. The culmination of a year's worth of growing is the *Green Blade* now in your hands.

This season, the humble potato is the feature vegetable of the *Blade*, showing up in poetry and prose as a symbol of love and sustenance. And it is these, the fundamental emotions like love, fear, and loss that we consume daily, that consume us and that root themselves in our writing. Peg Bauernfeind's essay "Pomme de Terre" celebrates romantic love, while Betty Benner's poem "Love Story" honors the love particular to a grandmother for her grandchild. In contrast, Nancy Hengeveld's poem "Headline" explores how raw fear can be the catalyst for change.

Thanks, always, to Dean and Sally Harrington for their hard work and dedication in seeing the RAWC through a year of transition, and for having the vision to want to grow the programming to create a stronger writing community. A sincere thank you to all the contributors to the *Green Blade*, as well as a hearty welcome to Nicholas Ozment as he joins the Editorial Board.

The *Green Blade* has changed publishers, and we'd like to thank Tom Driscoll for providing us an alternate, local publishing avenue through his indie publishing house Shipwreckt Books. We are very excited about this new partnership.

And a special thank you to Melissa Lammers for the cover art *Uisge Braugh*. Melissa showed her paintings and sculptures at the Greenwood Prairie Art Gallery in 2014, and two of her magnificent paintings have found a permanent home in the RAWC lobby. They are worth a trip to see in person, if you haven't already.

And now, for the main course. Just like the growing of potatoes, we've gotten a little dirt under our fingernails in the process of putting together this issue of the *Blade*--writing, revising, editing, and getting the layout right. The *Green Blade* is our potato, really—unpretentious, comfort food. Local and satisfying.

So, pull up a chair. You'll need salt and pepper, a pat of butter or a little gravy. Chew slowly. Experience the thrill of literary consumption. And, as a side note, the *Green Blade* pairs equally well with hot tea, dark coffee, and cookies.

Poetry

On this cool night, I want to slip in
Su Smallen

Bed beside you, in that way we so easily fit,
Tuck my chill feet between your warm,
Like you love, and tell how it was today,

To hear Joyce recite Dickinson in rushes,
Tracking the dewy field. *Death will stop for me*
And you, but only after I die with you,
Without haste, toward eternity.

Marriage Suite
Dan Butterfass

XXVIII

Like a sundial
we slowly turn away
until we're in cold shadow
then inch back toward
one another's warmth. Home

from my canoe trip, your limbs
are strong as water rippling its moist
light over the light-grey skin
of shoreline cedars. You in your perennial
gardens, me following my bird dog's wake
through the morning woods, we separate
like a braided creek, yet remain
one creek all the way upstream
and one all the way down. This
wooden boat of our years doesn't leak
with its fresh coat of paint
and little repairs. We close

the cabin in fall, leaving the stereo on,
and return in spring to music
that's reveled in itself all winter.

Morning Love
Melissa McNallan

She loved the way his eyes
focused in on hers and
the curve of his lips and
how she couldn't turn--

Whining of milk being steamed for
another mocha-latte-cappuccino-whatever.

He loved the way her voice
could be so soft and
assured and
the gentle way she saw--

Grinding of coffee being blended into
liquid candy for the can't-be-bothered-to-acquire-a-taste set.

What? He had to ask her. And again.
She watched his focus get lost
to the barista's holler of names
as she tried to tell him how she loved morning.

Proposal
Nicole Borg

Summer break has our pockets full of teaching money—
this is our first stop—a fishing town,
built on steep hills and water's smooth edge,
feels more like New England than California surf.

We decide against camping, get a room at The Anchor
two blocks from the ocean. We stroll the boardwalk
past paint-peeled boats and quiet gift shops.
Salt wind blows my hair in both our faces.

The Rock is a mesmerizing giant, rugged island,
humped and leathery-back of water troll,
beautiful in afternoon sun. I point to a narrow road.
I want to get married on that rock.

He laughs and pulls me to him.
At a restaurant on the water, we order shrimp
and white wine and eat too much. We speak
in undulating tones, our sandals, toe-to-toe under the table.

We go for a walk after dark, buy microbrews
from a frowning corner store. Outside, light ascends from
humid ocean air, I taste rain on the breeze.
Fog moves in like silence, fringes of dream.

At the motel, the T.V. doesn't work. We lie in bed
and imagine our wedding—the white cathedral in San Diego.
Soft rain and thrash of waves lull him to sleep.
In darkness, I kiss his forehead and listen to his even breath.

8

Choreography for a Life: First 38 Years
Nicole Borg

Dedicated to SHS Class of 1994

We can't slow the dance—
Earth's perfect pirouette
and courting her partner;
She, regal and blue;
He, all flash and heat;

revolving so slowly we forget—
breathe wishes and count stars,
clap at a rowdy meteor show,
the seductive wink of an eclipse.

Days and years and space
immeasurable,
we could almost believe—
we know better.

From the mirror, our laugh lines
dance around our mouths,
the etching by our eyes,
new landscape of our bodies
that have led and followed
many partners to many beats.

Above us, still, the stars,
the Great Possibility, dreams
waiting for us to incline our heads.
And tonight, those friends

who remember us. Us,
the beautiful critics, dreamers,

brave fools, bright-eyed clowns,
children impatient to enter the world,
its promise, its song.

We move in time with this season,
taking the hands of our loves
      and step—
                         This longing
as if for spring comes. The air crisp
with ponderosa and lodgepole,
spruce and fir, bittersweet notes of fall.

The black night spills stars
and the heavy gem of the moon set deep
in the socket of space can only offer us
dreamy silver light and whisper
      don't wait.

Dear K.,
Nicole Borg

You keep your cats.
Having a man is overrated. Even on those
lonely nights, the cats will give better comfort,
a quiet understanding or cry with you in *yaos*
of feline sorrow. The boyfriend who spurned you
all those years ago, they would gladly claw his eyes out.
What can a man offer to equal that?

Maybe you thought you'd have children.
Not with the boy who lit his school on fire and
went to Juvie. A nice boy, from church,
and your kids would look like tiny blonde
versions of him, but with less body hair.

You never thought you'd have forty-two cats.
That you'd build a house just for them,
clawing posts and cat hostels, hidden passageways
and secret rooms for their kitty trysts. You imagine
feline love affairs throughout the house—
at least someone is *getting some*, you think.

I say, keep the cats—your mom is pleased
to be a kitty-Grandma, she never wanted grandchildren.
And you'll be happier by far caring for them,
doting on them, cleaning up after them
than some dog-faced man.

Love,

N.

Talking to the Dead
Nicole Borg

The scuttling in the attic
does not sound animal—
when I climb up there's old insulation,
inches of dust and this heaviness
     I can't shake.

Someone has been trying
for weeks to send me a message—
pyramids of coins stacked neatly
in corners, lamps turned on
I know I've shut off, my car keys
missing, toast crumbs on the counter
make the profile of a face.

I mailed one letter to the dead—
Send this to ten people
you love the most, and please,
     don't forget me.

Soft Voice
Susan McMillan

Life is new our first summer up north on the farm.
This cold, tree-lined Michigan sky seems frozen
a bottomless blue, while July wind through pines
blows a tune like winter. Dark green grass grows
tall in ditches that trace our wild forty-acre plot
of field, alder, swamp, cedar, stone.

After being cooped up in the city—tiny, dust-dry
lawn and house with three small bedrooms to hold
eight bodies—this free space we now own seems
unending. A gate suddenly swings wide and all
six of us kids head for verdant pasture, free
to wander in any direction, spread out for good.

My first taste of aloneness addicts me to privacy,
liberty, total unfettered autonomy— indulgences
from which I cannot recover. I learn self-expression
through the soft voice of nature and a simple pen.
My entire life, I may never know what it means
to feel lonely.

Tenderfoot
Susan McMillan

Small and superficial
my knowledge of the prairie,
not much to draw from
though once I crossed from Red Wing
twelve hundred miles west
to Rocky Mountain foothills, plucked

with hungry eyes through dirty windows
autumn stems of undulating gold,
fell in love. My Amtrak carried feet
were only whooshed above the grasses,
not tramped through sod
like boots of dogged pilgrims

and their oxen-pulled carts,
or bison-hide moccasins
of Arikara, whose day-to-day
existence lay forged in each expression
of the prairie's quiet face.
Too little remains—
deep roots sacrificed
to reckless scoop and spade of modern greed,
bluestem and dogtooth daisy sold
in plastic pots to suburb hobby gardeners
for so-called native landscape plots,
my own sad self grown up among them.

I tuck damp roots of prairie smoke
and winking blue-eyed grass between
rough clumps of joe pye weed
along my fresh clipped lawn—
this little patch I cultivate

restrained and insufficient.

True prairie needs vastness.
In sleep, I wade wide seas
of waist high windblown verdure,
taste green and wiry stems
through broken skin
of two bare feet.

Know-Nothing
Emilio DeGrazia

All that calm water on lakes
With waves rippling ashore
Says nothing to me—
So I can't make sense

Of those schools of fishes
Lurking big-mouthed below
Like numb thoughts in dreams
Running nowhere in my mind.

And the shrill sun beaming
Its fires so brilliantly at me
I can't stare down, to ask
What it thinks, believes or knows,

What light it can shed
On war, suffering or love,
Or if the leaves of autumn trees
Are more clueless than oilmen

Because trees never learned to work
And squawk, because they never complain
That no one makes sense of them
From behind the windshields of cars,

And because trees, like galaxies,
Concoct no theories and theologies,
Just being there swirling or still,
Mindless and beautiful.

Living Inside-Out
Emilio DeGrazia

For him there's more to it than digging in
To rid himself of garbage and trash,
Or channeling the latest flood of news
Into sewers that disappear inside his house,

Or to say no again and again and again
To the one walking by, the one out of sight,
As she follows him home to his bed
Without waking the woman asleep next to him,

Or to release the rage for what's real and true
From behind the cathedral brow of belief
Where doubts widen the cracks between stones
Without letting a touch of light shine through.

He looks for the face of his father in a crowd,
And promises his mother he'll never leave her.
He extends smiles and handshakes all around
As noise makes the rounds looking for rhymes.

He tries to shake off the leashes he's on,
And sees both sides with two eyes, too late.
Nearby is a lake he never knew as a boy.
With no fear of drowning he swims naked in it.

Living Outside-In
Emilio DeGrazia

The diesel of busses and trucks dizzies his legs.
When he noses for the odors of bare-limbed trees
The stench of battlefield corpses
Enters naves through cracks in stained glass.

Daily a new woman appears at his door.
The lines on her face are familiar and strange.
She desires to make love by entering him,
Then writes her name on his mirror, and leaves.

He brings the random into his schemes, the egret
Standing on one leg in a backwater swamp
Shimmering with the blues of diesel alchemy
While atoms and galaxies dance on, unseen.

He sits still enough to see one leaf
And one stone happening on the grass.
He makes eye contact with one face in a crowd.
He finds the stone in the face, the face in the leaf.

They tell a story about losses and loves.
Wisps begin arriving, whisperings and scents
That drop hints at him about losses and loves.
He waits for the words of hints to enter him.

At the Hardware Store
Kit Rohrbach

I come for parts
to fix what's broken.
Like a magpie, I gather
shiny metal pieces
I'd forgotten I needed.

The man in the plumbing aisle
has my father's hands--
brown spotted, long fingered,
careful in the way he opens his wallet
knowing his money must last
for all time,
knowing there is not much left
of either,
but still buying a washer
to stop a faucet dripping.

I leave the store
with a heart
I'd forgotten was broken.

Bad Morning
Kit Rohrbach

My cup tipped over
onto my foot
so now not only
do I have no coffee,
but my toes are scalded
and my shoe is wet.

You gave me a poem
I do not like.
Should I ask you
to rewrite it?
repair the syntax?
rearrange the imagery?
refill my cup?

I can't decide
what to do because
my shoe is wet,
my foot hurts,
I have no coffee,
and there is such expectation
in your eyes.

Lorraine
Kit Rohrbach

In the pocket
of her navy blue dress,
the one
with small white dots
and a small white collar,
there's a picture
of a perfect kitchen
where the cupboards are full,
the dishes clean,
the drawers tidy,
where voices are hushed
in prayers of grace
and beer is not spilled
on the floor.

She tore this dream
from a magazine
in the clinic's waiting room
when no one was looking,
and only the kicks
inside her belly
to object.

She imagines
sealing the kitchen
in a card
to give to her child
to show her intentions
were good.

Headline
Nancy Hengeveld

This is what it's like:
One day you wake up to a foot of snow,
the next, to kids in tee shirts
throwing snowballs at the bus stop.

Then, days of sun, people everywhere,
strollers, bikes, kites, rakes.

Two days later, the schools are closing,
and there you are, shivering in a cotton dress,
sliding around on the sidewalk in your sandals.
You have to leave work early, drive home on ice.

You dig out your boots and mittens,
make soup, turn on the heat,
listen to the weather report.
But you don't want to believe it.
Sometimes they're wrong.

It goes on like that, so you don't dare plan a picnic.
You can't plant seeds.

There's that promise of change,
the memories of flowers.

That's why you stay.

Until one day you see the headline: Homicide.
You read.

You think: That could have been me.
Last night.
I could have been killed.

That's when you leave.

Protection 101
Nancy Hengeveld

You can hear the soft clucking of a wild turkey
tending her brood in the woods,
but you can't see them.
You hardly ever see them,
with their camouflage of feathers,
invisible in the brush.

It's like that, every time you recognize
a certain sound,
a distinct smell,
that feeling someone's there.

Children feel it, too.

Watch them recoil
from a kiss, a touch
and let them go,
with wings outspread,
brown feathers
disappearing
in the brush.

Rain Running
Jennifer Jesseph

Here we are
running in rainbows
running in rain
rain running
funning, children
with the huff and puff
of youth
running

Rain Running

Dance in the rain
Prance in the rain
Come along, come along
Grace in the rain
Wet face in the rain
running and running
we chase in the rain

Rain Running

Come, let's go running.
The sun isn't sunning.
The sky isn't drying
and some say it's crying
but I know it's raining
and dripping and draining.

Come, let's go splashing
and mud puddle smashing.
Forget about rain boots!
Just hubbub and hoot hoots.

These wet drippy sky days
are more fun than dry days.

Come, let's get soaking,
a rain drenching joking.
Torrential deep laughter
is just what I'm after.
Let thunder be thunder
and lightning and wonder.

Our parents won't mind us.
They might even find us.
Their laughter will bubble
and splash away trouble.
We'll all just go running
and slipping and funning
and laughing and wetting
and never regretting.

I Love Your Funny, Funny Face
Patricia Barone

1.
I love your funny, funny face
as you crouch in the back seat
with your wax false teeth
jaunting out your upper lip
so speeding cars would jerk,
heads whipping round—
One truck gunned backward
skidding the yellow line off the road
to see you again. By then you were not
over-biting but primly smiling—
just the swipe of a leer.

You were pleased to suppose
some little girl would
make up a story—
how the wolf man could
retract his fangs.

2.
"Hoodiboodiba," and "cha cha cha,"
your nonsense gift of tongues for children.
Our toddler imitates your cadence,
As you cake-walk, rock and roll
till the needle jumps.
   We need the street
for your Jackson-5 strut,
that Mardi Gras step on Elysian Fields.

You mock your middle-aged gut,
balloon it under your chest and whoosh it
down with a slap on your belt.

Matt laughs, so you bend your knees,
Whisk knuckles on the floor as his gorilla.

3.
Your father crossed his eyes
and stuck his tongue between his teeth.
When was my dad absurd? Germanic, he'd say,
"Life is a serious business; we start dying
on the day we're born."

Since our marriage, I've lost the dark family
circles beneath my eyes. A missing abscessed tooth
gives my face a goofy gape I don't replace it.
It's part of loving you   to want a funny face.

A First Weaving
Patricia Barone

Claire's small fingers push down
a row of yellow with her comb.
She hides her face in the yarn bag
looking for blue, and my mother,
quick, pulls the last thread taut,
smoothing Claire's sticky knots.

Claire catches her at it.
—"I'll do it myself!
Myself!" And Grandma bristles.
—"I only want to help!"
—"I have to do it my way!"
Claire doesn't know how
to weave, but she's bound to do it,
toiling, forcing weft through warp
skipping three strands together
in her haste to finish.

She must weave this scarf today
before we leave for the *Altenheim*,
Christmas a far off country
for Claire and for Great-Aunt Hilaire,
who waits in a summer gazebo,
and doesn't recall who we are.

I know my mother is hurt.
that my child isn't weaving for her
on the loom she herself bestowed
for Claire's seventh birthday.

Claire wets the yarn with her tears:
"I'll never get it right!"

Grandma snorts. "You don't have to
do it if it makes you miserable,
and everyone around you!"

"Oh, no," Claire cries, "I'm stopped!"
We grownups watch her snarl a *cul de sac*,
half the threads hanging slack.
"My grandma was the last," says Grandma,
"to spin, but my mother used to weave."
Claire stops crying—Grandma seems to know
how one loop locks another in.

Grandma threads the reeds, telling Claire:
"Pretend the top threads are your mother,
and the bottom threads are me.
You are the shuttle, your only job
is to carry the wool through this shed."

Passing the shuttle to each other,
Together we fold the weft
back and forth upon itself,
and the cloth begins to climb,
and the weft holds the warp and our girl.

My Shadows, Our Light
Patricia Barone

Last night I went back like a child.
I wept and was afraid, but not today.
You're here, you know I wake
to wander from room to room
until I'm cold in the attic bed
and can't get up again.

I needed to travel to shadows
flicking the ceiling, birds wings
in a barn, to listen as my loft
settled true on your breathing.

Now our glass globe swings
to gather in our room, rocking slow,
the bell cord steady on first morning light,
the silk of rain so blue, only skin is warm.

The Mauve Mummy
Nicholas Ozment

The museum curator paid a good price,
even though the skull was shattered.

"Unique," he marveled. Unique, indeed.
The mummy's wraps were stained

head to toe with a mysterious dye.
Mauve. Color of sunset. I did not tell him

that it was I who crushed its cranium
with the curved edge of a crowbar.

I also failed to mention that, just before
we resealed its ancient casket

to haul it from its silent crypt,
the mouth of the mauve mummy *moved*.

Brainy Conversation
Nicholas Ozment

Late last night as I lingered
in a place I was not supposed to be,
it was my fortune to overhear
the conversation
of two brains in a jar.

"We," said the first brain,
"being cored from our craniums
and yet still being lucid,
are the greatest miracle of science."

"That," replied brain number two,
"is nothing. While we yet
resided in our former skulls,
we were the greatest miracle
of nature."

I could not help but interject.

"It is a wonder," I said,
"that you have no lips or larynx
or lungs, and yet you speak."

"Visitor," said the second brain,
"Corollary to my previous point,
it is a greater wonder that we ever spoke."

I would like to have stayed
and talked philosophy, metaphysics,
even favorite jokes with the brains,
but I did not want to be caught
and perchance share their fate.

Yet today I have walked about
filled to the brim with awe,
to think that I see the world
from a jar balanced precariously
on the uppermost point
of a delicate spine,
   wonderful as a spider's web,
   fearsome as a snake.

lint
Dee Bezoier

spirit
through-sounds as
per-son

like lint
found everywhere

as per-son dies
death
becomes life

from parentheses
freed

tiny
Dee Bezoier

tiny lunchbox
in
tinier grip

steps so small

a stumbling march
to wait

within sight of
how it was

oops
Dee Bezoier

negatories

rhetorically coerce
to
effect denial

like miniscule ritual murders
substituting
place-holding Corpses for
noetic breath

… or Not?

Stalemate
Kate Halverson

the state in which one player —
(spouse, child, parent or friend)
comes to a draw—can't win

further action and/or progress
by opposing parties
impossible

the war had reached a stalemate—
transitive verb [object of a noun]
bringing to or causing THE END

the state she woke up in
a game played between two parties
backed into opposing corners

divorce ridiculous fights worthless
change unheard of except in novels
and so it was she put down her book

remembering all she'd dreamed of
picked up her pen and began to
write — filling her well
with all that was good

the same way he filled his—
spotting the moon rise

the inseparable two
home alone now

a peaceful man
and his devoted wife

determined *not* to be stale—
still looking for fun
amongst the hum-drum

Page Turner
Betty J. Benner

When she saw the magnifying machine looming large on my kitchen table, a friend who is sometimes confused about words said to me, "I'm sorry you have immaculate degeneration."

Ink and paper
Are more than tools of the trade.
They are essential life components,
Have grown to be so
Over the course of eighty years.
The sight of black letters,
The grainy feel of paper,
The special smell that an aged volume brings.
Diminished sight does not have to mean
Losing a world, they say.

Listen to talking books, they say.
The machine sits, box unopened,
Next to a stack of catalogs, updated monthly,
While I slide the real thing,
Life after Life, by Kate Atkinson,
Under the magnifier taking over
The kitchen table.
I set the type size up to six,
Read the final page the day before
Book club meets.
With eyesight decreasing,
It takes longer and longer
To transfer what the pages say
To my brain.

Then there's the problem of
What to do with the shelves of books

40

And stacks of them piled in corners.
What to do about not recognizing people.
(Faces are blurred, eyes are fuzzy and colorless,
Mouths turn up at the left corner)
The degeneration is macular,
Not so much immaculate.
She turns a new page.

Marbles, a game
Betty J. Benner

I remember marbles,
Kept a drawstring bag,
Cat's eyes and puries
And one twice the size of the others
Was the shooter.
We drew a circle
In sand,
In dirt,
On the sidewalk,
Or made one of string on the rug.
Using thumbnail and knuckle
On the shooter
We would aim to hit
The other person's marbles
And add them to our collection.
I stopped playing the game as I grew,
But kept the marbles
In the drawstring bag
For many years.

A friend I had not seen
Since the old days
Came to visit.
She had helped me through the rough times.
As we whispered our goodbyes,
She said, "I'm glad
You haven't lost your marbles."
Later I retrieved the bag, opened it,
And counted them. Twelve, there were,
Cat's eyes and puries.
And one shooter.

To a Lost Poem
Betty J. Benner

I had you cornered
Last night as I waited for sleep.
Each word, though not a pearl,
Finding its place with the others,
Being what I wanted to say
Or give form to.
Sleep called
As I reckoned how
I would get you down
In ink, on paper.

Where did you go?
Slipped away, you did,
After all my groping in the dark.
Go, be with your brothers and sisters.
My spiral notebook invites others.
Sleep will not slip them away.
Would that I could
Learn not to corner you;
Or get you down,
But to write you into freedom,
Into winging your own way.

Love Story
Betty J. Benner

She reads the day's emails, browses the Internet,
As is her custom on quiet evenings.
A documentary catches her eye,
Four young men tell their stories.
Transgender stories. How they arrived—
And how they have always been--
Where they are now.

She looks closer. Moves closer to the screen.
The one young man with the blonde curls
Wearing the flowered shirt
Is her grandson.
There is no doubt.
He is earnest and quiet in his statements.

He flies from New York to Minnesota
For the 2014 winter holiday,
Sits on the floor of his mother's apartment,
Stroking Ophelia the cat
After the meal
Shared by his grandmother's family,
All present but one.

She sits next to him. They speak
Of his younger days, not so very long ago,
She recalls his Virginia high school graduation.
She mentions a prom photo of him—
Beautiful red gown, high heeled sandals,
Hair to the shoulders.
He looks at her for a moment, then
Says in a low voice,.
"Throw it away. Toss it out."

Later at home she looks for the photo.
It has disappeared.
Instead, she places his framed 2014 holiday photo
On the kitchen windowsill.
Visible as she eats her meals,
A daily reminder
Of a loving grandchild
And her love for him.

To a Fault
Tim J. Brennan

Dead moths lie crumpled
beneath a black twill suit hanging
in a dark closet—

short change confetti from a time
when people thought about longings
but never spoke to until all bones
ossified from misuse

Ash Wednesday
Tim J. Brennan

For at least another year I am the blind's dog
who turns his nose to the wind and allows
forehead ash to enter my blood

I dare not dream, not of the sea
not of the past, nor of houses
with closed doors

Wild Berries

Tim J. Brennan

The woods near my home, the place where I learned
to place a finger over Dana's nipple in such a way
she would sigh, were filled with wild berries

Dana would put one to her mouth, dipping
in her gray tee much like a young brown otter
through water, sliding into thick bank chicory
filled with yellow finches just watching us

In Lieu of Flowers

Ken McCullough

for Mary Lynn, on Valentine's Day, 2015

I
Outside these windows in the darkest night
we hear a barred owl, not a nightingale,
incessant in our twisted old maple--
comfort to you, but harbinger to me.
The candle by the bed is guttering.
I hear you muttering in your sleep--
we both have dreams that almost wear us out;
then we wake, to a world stumbling in harness.
The light comes through the curtains, your eyes smile--
your toothy grin, sunny disposition
always fill every room you occupy.

II
Our house on the bluffs, may someday crumble,
we'll let the heavy fences fall and rot.
The fires in our bellies will have banked
to a bed of embers, but still burn hot.
Across these fields we wander in the dark
the splash of stars, the velvet petals fall.
I faintly hear young Puck a-singing.
The shaggy heads of peonies, browning
at the edges, mined by ants, purple-blue,
misconstrue and slumber, too. I lived all
those years without you, and now another
life, but deeper, begins again today.

Socket
Ken McCullough

I know you are the one who wrote the book,
you, the one who always picks up the check.
When I heard your voice all my senses shook,
unlocked my chains, a bushel and a peck
of the rhymes lined up for the slaughter.
You were naked except for blue knee hose
on an island swirling in red water.
Today, ten years later, I dip my toes
in the sea. I should have known you were right,
always, as the pelicans fly in low.
I never wanted to put up a fight;
in your presence, there is no ebb and flow.
I gave in back then and am still giving.
Thank you for this blessing, for forgiving.

Avebury
Ken McCullough

I

At the end of the serpentine hill
our car broke wind in the village.
Couples cloaked in tweed
with Horlick's on the brain.
A woman with an old cigar:
I understood the hood
and the blue uterine breath
and the eye rolled back in the head
reflecting sky. In the apse
of the chapel at the center
stood God, that old recluse,
taking sherry at midday.

II

We walked west and rested
at the serpent's tail. Came back
for sandwiches where heads more
fluid, more divine than broken
had stood these stones in circles.
Ensorceled by the berm, we spun
each other, and the white wine
was reddened by the sun. Our bodies
beat as one. Bodies. Beat as one.

III

As you crossed the stile, I admired
the turn of calf and sweet behind
beneath your gold and russet skirt.

Up the avenue of broken stones--pitted
male molars, discolored female eyeteeth,
wet grass, the pasture full of Guernseys--
we stepped between green manure.
You, skeptic, my queen being,
called softly once and the whole herd
bolted, frantic, breaths wreathing,
eyes wide, surrounding you, awaiting
your command. The embarrassed goddess,
you dismissed them with a flick
of your wrist. Had I not been there...

IV

Hand in hand, out past the sounds
where a nest hung pendulous,
we crossed the fence to thicket
where you undid me, turned me
quick and startled into a stag
with hound and huntsmen closing.

Womanesque
Ken McCullough

You were unforgettable
though I can't recall your name
I remember every dip and tip
haven, harbor, slip
the exact temperature at
blush of evening
grove and savannah
flocks in the shoals
hands like large waterbirds
asleep in the gray moors of your eyes
pulled me down and moored me
in the buzzing of your voice
your laughter was uncanny
like a zebra out of sequence
your feet for swimming
and you could charm
the sting from a scorpion

Young Love
Peter Allen

My buddy and I were vandalizing
real estate signs in a nearby woods soon to be
destroyed for the sake of money, epitomized
by model homes advertizing the good life carved
from a stand of trees growing ever since colonial
white men came to what would be called
Gaithersburg in MD. We were young and bored
in High School, proceeding down the continuum
with alacrity and, yes, we were drinking too, which
I liked even better than walking through the
trembling woods which progress was about to rip
apart for cash. We painted "Bull Shit Model"
on every placard that betrayed our notion of decorum.

The way light was shining on a pond made me have
two shadows, front and back, one from the moon and
one reflected from the water we found when we stumbled to
Isaac Walton's sanctuary. Was I surprised when she
was tall and beautiful rising from the mist like a mermaid
except she had two feet. I was young when I handed her
a towel and she was smiling.

Next morning I was not so young
and when I got home my
Mother wept because of me.

A Harem of Potatoes
Peter Allen

Keep them in the dark.
They need to be dry
at room temperature.
Don't wash until ready
to be cooked.

Cultivation requires
mounding dirt in rows.
As the plants grow larger,
cover with soil from
between the rows.

If potatoes get any sunlight,
they turn green and bitter.
They'll grow eyes
on the dining room table.

Harvesting requires
dirty hands groping
in loose soil for little
ones the garden fork missed.
Place gently in storage.

Proper care is
rewarded with potato
bounty. Don't wash.
Put in a dark, cool place.
They'll wait for you.

Potato Garden
Steven R. Vogel

You showed me into your garden toward evening,
the sun chased off behind marauding purple
    and castaway pink.

Red clover swelled its perfume in the hollow,
    spilled it up the ridge in humid layers.
With the turning breeze, chive and garlic flowers
    and the green fuzz of tomato churned back.

Your countenance betrays
a joy unspoken.
The sounds of you
ablate the call of night.

Your garden is set in mounds (you never said why),
undulating, fertile rounds of loam, evenly spaced,
each one the shadow of another,
    a shadow for what lies below:

ovoid, lush, succulent fruits, cobbled together,
    beholden to the earth,
        pure, weeping flesh, kept white in the close dust.

How hidden are your gentle parts!
How sacred your potentials!
Your peaceable generations
sleep with hushed vigor.

In haste of day, they are shoveled through—stung on the blade.
Can we do such violence?
Rummage below with quickening fingers, toes.

tumble them out, pet them free.
    And dirt, and dirt, and dirt.

This one, these two, we dash across our thighs.
They sing to our lips, carry crunching grit to our teeth.
    Dirt, and dirt, and dirt.

    But for water,
    we would have mud pie ...
    oh! water is within!
    Pump it freely!

The fresh of the evening:
    aching violet surrounds fuchsia;
    the catbird banished to a limb, just there.
Tiny witnesses betray the fertile flounces of the soil.

We left our shoes, our socks, what clothing we could,
    on the corner post—our only sentry.
It is cool, what touches me above;
it is warm, what touches below.

    Your staid silhouette
    suffers in the fade.
    The fog of your heat
    brushes by in wisps.

The rattled ground yields tuber strays
    to massage our several feet,
and each fumbling step interprets a breath,
    spending it out in fragments.

Dig down, comingle our soft parts.
I will creep upon your flesh, rearrange to suit you.
    My own dirty smell is ready for yours,
                                damsel love—
the warm heart of the earth, small potatoes,
    and crisp eyes all around.

Prose

Pomme de Terre
Peg Bauernfeind

I purchased a greeting card with a picture of a Mickey Mouse character dressed in yellow, red and blue garb and wearing a black French fedora. Inside the card were the words, Pomme de terre.

Pomme de terre is French for potato, an apple of the earth. If you live in Minnesota, you may have planted potatoes. Around Easter time you visit the seed store and buy seed potatoes; you look for the eyes. At home you cube the spuds so each piece has an eye. On Good Friday you plant the eyes in a garden hole just so deep and you heap a dirt pile just so high. Then you wait and finally up come the green leaves. The leaves grow into vines and bear yellow and black beetles. You pick off the bugs and drown them in kerosene. When the vines dry up you dig up the hills and there lay the potatoes, red, yellow, white, blue or gold depending on your choice in the spring. Pomme de terre.

I bought the pomme de terre card for EJ's birthday. He is a potato man. Like the Potato Eater men in Van Gogh's painting, *The Potato Eaters,* EJ is a man of the earth.

Van Gogh wanted to depict peasants as they really were. He wanted to make it so that people get the idea that these folk, who are eating their potatoes by the light of their little lamp, have tilled the earth themselves with these hands they are putting in the dish, and so it speaks of manual labor and — that they have thus honestly earned their food.

Van Gogh would have liked EJ. He's hard working and honest. I met EJ at the Weaver Methodist Church sort of by chance. I was curious about a congregation that gave a thousand dollars to the local humane society. I've got a dog, Woody.

EJ grew up on a farm on a bluff above Weaver. He stood me up on our first date. I didn't get mad; many of my friends are forgetful. Later he admitted to being scared, my being new to the church. But on our second date he drove me around Weaver. A tour of Weaver takes five minutes with three minutes to spare. EJ's tour of Weaver took us across the old Highway 61 Bridge to the Whitewater River, past the Weaver Methodist Church, the closed-up hotel that once housed an art gallery, the blacksmith shop and the boarded-up school building. Weaver also had the first concrete highway in the state, Minnesota 74 from Weaver to Elba.

A hundred years ago Weaver thrived as a booming river town with hotels, a railroad station, two merchandise stores and a post office. EJ remembered three gas stations. Two on the highway had electricity but at the third station you hand-pumped the gas into a dome at the top of the rig and let gravity fill up your gas tank. EJ also remembered that George at the Weaver tavern had free game feeds on Friday nights— deer, coon, fish or geese—whatever the hunters brought in. EJ said he could buy a beer for a nickel.

Folks from around the area drove their cattle to Weaver. They supplied the Chicago markets with beef, fish, geese, ducks, cabbages, potatoes and melons. The one thing the folks didn't export was their kids. Every family had at least a dozen or so. The kids stayed around Weaver and married their neighbors. Today there are about twenty families in Weaver, but those families have roots co-mingled like hills of potatoes, apples of the earth.

For example, one day in the Weaver Church kitchen, Bonnie, who's not from Weaver either, and I were drinking coffee. I'd say we were gossiping too, but neither of us knows anyone. A young gal walked in. I asked her name and she said, "I'm Kelly, Marion's daughter. Marion lives up the road next to the Showalters who bought the old Martin farm." I remember looking at Bonnie and her looking at me. We nodded. I wanted to tell Kelly, "I haven't a root in the valley. I'm alien," but I didn't want to scare her away. I remembered new folks are scary.

EJ is a Weaver potato, but he's not a couch potato. He just turned 81. He's older than me but in ways younger. He volunteers as an angel at the St. Elizabeth's Hospital pushing wheel chairs and greeting folks coming through the doors to see doctors. He exercises in the cardiac rehab and carries on with one of the blond trainers like he's forty. He just bought a new car, drives too fast, plays cards, and bowls on Friday with his Senior League. His favorite food is mashed potatoes with gravy.

We've been best friends for two years. Potatoes are a big deal between us. If EJ did the cooking, we'd have potatoes and gravy three times a week with leftovers on Tuesdays and Thursdays.

I try not to scare EJ anymore. He doesn't like my cooking—pasta, tomatoes and veggies. Like I said, I haven't made mashed potatoes and gravy just on principle. He's smart though. He didn't finish high school, something to do with throwing a snowball, but he saw the world with the Navy.

EJ is dearer to me than potatoes. Van Gogh knew about potato eaters. His masterpiece reveals a wholly different way of life. Van Gogh painted the potato eaters' hands gnarled and coarse from digging potatoes. He made them friendly, sharing a meal together, all ages. And only Van Gogh paints a potato that shimmers and shines. It's the same feeling I get when I'm with EJ. He's an apple of the earth discovered in Weaver. I'm glad I found him. He's my pomme de terre.

Waste Rituals
Emilio DeGrazia

My father, an Old Country immigrant, had a ritual. He left the dishwashing to my sisters and the drying to me, but after every meal he routinely escaped to the garden in back with a handful of leftovers— potato peels, eggshells, apple cores, bean tips, and other debris dirt likes to eat. There he'd dig a little hole with his spade and bury the stuff.

It is a sin to waste, he routinely said with a sad little shake of his head. Not only that: The buried stuff would turn into lovely tomatoes, eggplant, and beans next year.

He's gone now, so he won't have to put up with my wasteful ways. One of them is that I keep forgetting to use the reusable cloth bag in the back seat of my car. Again and again I find myself in the grocery store checkout line with the clerk asking me if I want paper or plastic. I always say paper, quietly bewildered by my failure to remember to reach into the back seat for the reusable bag, while feeling morally superior to those lugging their groceries away in plastic bags.

The plastic bags disappear, while adding up. By the millions, billions. They're thin but tougher than nails, refusing to rust away when we have no further use for them. They're an invisible and weighty waste problem that, unlike my father's handful of leftovers, don't usefully go away.

Millions—maybe billions—of people would make feasts of our throw-away food. According to the Society of St. Andrew, an organization dedicated to feeding America's hungry, more than twelve billion (12,000,000,000) pounds of food was wasted in the first two months of 2013. If we multiply those two months worth of waste by ten remaining months we achieve a gross tonnage difficult to find room for in our minds. Of all food harvested in the U.S. less than 50% gets eaten, this in a nation where obesity is a serious health issue.

Waste's ability to increase and multiply makes it a significant growth industry. The EPA reminds us that "food leftovers are the single largest component of the waste stream by weight in the United States." A National Resource Defense Council study (2012) shows that, "Getting food to our tables eats up 10 percent of the total U.S. energy budget, uses 50% of U.S. land, and swallows 80 percent of fresh water consumed in the U.S." And here's another turn of the screw: It costs about one billion dollars per year to get rid of food we don't eat. As talk about the impact of government spending on future generations heats up I wonder if we're feeding our children to the monstrous waste we wallow so neatly in.

Think of what a field day my father's eggplants, tomatoes, and beans would have with all our leftovers.

He had a hard time throwing anything away. He'd find a neat little place in the basement or garage for pieces of pipe and wire, for old boards, engine parts, and used bricks, for coffee cans full of nuts and bolts and bent nails, and for empty coffee cans. When he needed to fix something he knew where to find the part that fit. Meanwhile, the EPA tells us that Americans generate about 250 million tons of Municipal Solid Waste daily, or 4.43 pounds of MSW per person per day.

Researchers at the Lawrence Livermore Laboratory also add their bits of information about the waste Americans pile up. LLNL flow charts show that "more than half (58%) of the total energy produced in the U.S. is wasted due to inefficiencies, such as waste heat from power plants, vehicles, and light bulbs...And while residential, commercial and industrial sectors waste about 20% of their energy, the transportation sector wastes a full 75%, making it 25% energy efficient."

It's a lot harder, in short, for oil to move cars made of steel than for humans made of flesh and bones to use their feet. The cars we ride in get a free ride at our expense, and they steer clear of the troubles caused by oil in the Mideast.

We vaguely know these grim facts, if not the actual numbers that are so huge we lose our minds in them. We know enough to turn off the lights, turn the thermostat down, walk or bike or carpool, eat smaller portions, recycle, bury leftovers into a compost pile, and lug our groceries home in a reusable bag.

But in my case there's a disconnect between what I know and what I do. I leave lights on, I drive when I could walk or bike, and I keep forgetting that reusable bag in the back seat of my car.

I wonder if I'm typical. I talk to myself about preventing waste, but my mumbling gets lost in all the noise I hear about "growth" and "jobs." In our national conversations about climate change and environmentalism I seldom hear the word "conservation" used, especially by "conservatives" whose arguments for fossil fuel growth are underwritten by fossil fuel industries. The case for "growth" and "jobs" is routinely made synonymous with "prosperity," but I seldom hear it linked to the poverty resulting from the expansion of waste. Nor are "growth" and "jobs" linked to the shrinkage of resources on a planet quietly experiencing population explosion. What I don't hear much about is also what I don't want to hear or do much about.

I'm not sure I forget that reusable bag in the back seat of my car because I'm losing my mind. I think that bag is not on my mind enough. When I talk to myself I usually can't remember what I said an hour ago. But when everyone's talking about the same thing it's hard to ignore what's being said. People like me need to tune into a new conversation about food, energy use and waste—call it a *national* conversation, one with the word *conservation* routinely used in it. Kids should learn to spell the word in their cradles, and older folks should utter it as they begin turning into eggplants, tomatoes, and beans too. Why do all the drilling, fracking, and pipelining to increase fossil fuel energy by 20% in the next ten years when we could reduce it, and much of the waste fossil fuels produce, by 20% in the next five? I don't think it would trouble us much to walk, bike, carpool, turn off some lights, watch less TV, drink from faucets rather than bottles and cans, and carry our groceries out in reusable bags.

The big industries that lobby for business as usual—and more "growth"—have indeed created habits that provide Americans an outstanding materialistic way of life made more enjoyable by sporadic outbursts of religiosity. But are these industries "growing" us to a breaking point, without making waste one of their deadly sins? How can the economy "grow" without turning our neighborhoods into gaseous landfills? The Chinese are wearing gas masks as they stroll down the avenues crowded with exhaustion pipes spewing out toxic fumes the winds are exporting to the U.S.

We need more talk—talk full of smart ideas and urgency—about waste's impact on prosperity. Can we more comprehensively figure the long-term and widespread costs of waste into our business calculations? How much more stuff do we need, and what can we do better without? Can we cut down on waste and increase prosperity by *de-materializing* our economy? Can we create both jobs and new wealth by professionalizing the relatively non-toxic and good work done by alternative health and human services providers, by educators and artists, by fix-it-up gurus, and by caretakers of culture and the environment? Would more people actually be happier in this leaner and cleaner economy? Would it save future generations of our children from the disasters business as usual profiteers are warning us about?

Certainly it would help if politicians and celebrities would speak out about this issue in a big way, but they're unlikely to do so until they hear a lot of us talking about it first.

I know I talk too much to myself, and it's one reason I so easily slip out of the habit of lugging my groceries home in a reusable bag. Every time I do that I almost realize that I've failed to translate my mind's preferences into the behaviors of everyday ritual. I've thought about buying more reusable bags and spreading them around the car so they're impossible to ignore, but that somehow rubs me wrong. I need a reusable ritual, not more reusable bags. Proper rituals, which conjure widespread commitment to norms that have special, even sacred, significance, are vital to the survival of a society. If I saw others routinely walking to the front door of the grocery store with reusable bags in hand, I'd be much more inclined to reach for mine in the back seat of my car. And I'd change other habits too, probably getting some good exercise riding the six blocks to the grocery store on my bike instead of in my car.

The Beginning of Words
P.S. Duffy

At the top of the page, the word "inflorescence" sat there to confuse him. Again. It's just a word, he told himself, as he thumbed through the pages.

Just a word. Like all the others. Countless words penciled in block letters at the tops of lined pages in the speckled copybooks at his feet. Words like "alabaster" and "ramshackle." And "jacaranda"— a tree they'd never seen and never would there in the backwoods of Maine. Words by themselves on some pages, on others followed by scratchings and cross-outs and more words below. Poems, maybe, though they didn't rhyme and there was no reason. None he'd ever seen, anyway. He never read them. Never asked to. They were her words, not his. "Phantom." "Imprisonment." "Omnipotence." Words piled on words. Stone borders between them.

But now he held them, pages of them, in his thick veined hands. Smudges, too, were there. A smear of blueberry, gooseberry—jams boiling overtime as she wrote down her words. Words preserved in a milky haze under a streak of paraffin on one page—or wax from the candle burned down to a nub before she blew it out. Him waiting upstairs in long johns for her to warm up the bed.

A filing of dirt sifted down from a binding. He collected it in the curl of his palm and thought of her strong arms, digging potatoes, and of earth's arms, now waiting. When had the words begun? Filling up her head, filling up copybooks, splayed out now on the floor by the sofa where she lay, wordless. What was the point of them? When did they begin? Not, surely, at the beginning of their time together. Years later, maybe—maybe as an escape from him. "Exile."

She clawed at the afghan. He adjusted it. Placed his hands on hers. Felt the restless fingering beneath. Got up then and fed the wood stove. Would keep it going all night so she'd be warm enough, though the summer air was soft. "Kindling" was a word she liked. And "dusk." Which he saw it was now. He resumed his seat, bent over, knees pressed against the sofa. Listened to the straggle of fevered breath. Watched the zig-zag afghan rise and fall, until it went still.

A scrap of a paper bag fell from the page of a copybook as the sky went velvet. He picked it up. A single word and a date: 1894. Smudged, too, it was, with a grease stain. From egg salad, it came to him with pounding certainty. From a picnic by the river some forty years before. She'd stretched her length, hands high along the rope, bare feet planted on the knot. The shriek of joy, the rush of her skirt as he'd pushed her out over the river. "Again!" she'd cried out when she sailed back to his arms, "again and again and again!"

He uncurled the scrap held now in his fist. Made himself re-read it. "Again!" A single word that held there all their beginnings. Written down on a shred of a grease-stained paper bag in 1894.

Dancing with Fred Astaire
Kit Rohrbach

Pneumonia. I'm 104 years old. Never been sick a day in my life and now I got pneumonia. I expect I'll get over it. You don't get to be 104 without being a tough old gal. And laying around in a hospital bed sure's not how I plan to spend the rest of my life. I'll be up and around again in a day or so but it was touch and go there for a while.

You know all them stories about how people who are dying see a long tunnel with light at the end of it and there's all the folks who have passed on before them? Well, it's like that and it ain't.

There's light all right, but not bright so you have to squint your eyes up. It's more like when the sun comes out after a heavy rain and part of the sky is still dark but there's blue peeking out in a few spots and making everything look clean. Not sparkly or nothing. Happy looking. All in all, I'd have to say it was just real pretty.

And there wasn't no tunnel. That was fine by me 'cause I never did like tunnels much, 'specially long ones. So I was glad to find a nice little stone bridge instead. There used to be a bridge like that not far from where I grew up and sometimes I'd go and drop sticks or walnut shells into the water on the upstream side, then run across to watch 'em float out from under the bridge and on down the creek. I'd make up all kinds of places they might end up in, like China or South America. And I'd wonder what some Chinaman would think when he saw a walnut shell come sailing by. Kids was more easily amused in them days, I guess.

So I was thinkin' I might do that again and was looking around for some sticks when who should come walking right up to me but Fred Astaire. Fred was a cat I had years and years ago. I knew he was dead and figured I must be dead too but I wasn't worried none about it. I was that glad to see him again. He was one of them black cats with a white patch on his chest that give him the look of being dressed up in a tuxedo. People thought that's why I called him Fred Astaire and I let 'em think it even though that wasn't the real reason at all. I called that

71

cat Fred Astaire because he loved to dance. He was doing it again there on that bridge, just like when he was alive. Winding in and out and around my ankles, lifting up his paws in prissy little steps and twitching his tail in time to some music only he could hear. And sometimes I could get to hearing the music too, and I'd scoop old Fred up in my arms and we'd waltz around the kitchen in big circles. I'd close my eyes and pretend I was all dolled up in a fancy ball gown and for a little bit I'd be as glamorous and beautiful as Ginger Rogers. I've had other cats since Fred but none of 'em liked to dance the way he did and I sure have missed him. It wasn't like Albert ever took me dancing.

Now it's a funny thing, but I'd no sooner had that thought about Albert than there he was, standing on the far side of the bridge and calling me to cross on over. And I started out to. But then I noticed he had that same look on his face like he always did. Sort of exasperated from trying to have patience with the world not coming up to his expectations. He hollered out, saying as how he'd been waiting awful long and I'd sure taken my sweet time about showing up. Well, I guess if he'd been waiting forty years, he had a right to be put out.

I'll tell you a secret. I wasn't sorry when Albert died. All our friends and neighbors come around to his funeral saying how sorry they was and I didn't say anything one way or the other. I just let 'em think what they wanted to think. That seemed like the best way and it made everybody happy.

So I was stalling around there on the bridge, petting Fred and trying to remember why it was I ever married Albert in the first place. I'd just about decided it was to get away from my mother when darned if she didn't shove Albert out of her way and start right in. It come as something of a surprise to me but people don't get no sweeter disposition just from being dead.

"Adelaide, stand up straight and quit slouching. Can't you do something with your hair? What is that you're wearing? I'm not having a daughter of mine looking like a floozy. And you might show some appreciation for all the things I've done for you."

That was my mother. Always doing things for me that I never wanted in the first place and then getting huffy 'cause I wasn't grateful enough. Like introducing me to her friends' pimply sons. That was prob'ly why I married Albert. He was the least spotty of the bunch and by the time he showed up my resistance was about worn down. She was still going on like she'd been saving it up all the years since she died.

"You've been nothing but a terrible disappointment to me. You never even gave me grandchildren and I had to make do with those disgraceful brats your brother John produced. I blame that woman."

Francine was a French girl that my brother met and married when he was over there in the Great War. Brought her home with him and it was a done deal without a by your leave to nobody. Mother never forgave either of them for that and she never called Francine by her name, just 'that woman'. But meeting Francine was somthin' of a revelation to me. She didn't give a snap of her fingers for all the things I'd been told were important, like never going out without a hat on. But the thing I liked best was the way her and John looked at each other, like they knew some secret the rest of the world wasn't in on. They was always together and when Francine died it wasn't but a couple of months before John followed right along after her.

I was getting the hang of this thing now so I started checking around for John and Francine. They was down along the edge of the water, John in his shirtsleeves and Francine with her shoes and stockings off, wading in the creek. They waved to me and I waved back and right about then it got to seeming like they was waving goodbye and I woke up in the hospital and maybe it was a dream. And maybe it wasn't. And if it wasn't, I'm real glad to know now how dying works. Sometimes it's easy to look back over the last hundred years and fret about the things I coulda done different. But I'm quits with that from now on. I'm gonna start thinking hard about all the people I'd like to meet on the other end of that bridge.

There was Olive Douglas. Everybody called her Dolly, and I met her when we was both working at Woolworth's and she was running the candy counter so she could afford to go to college. Real smart she was, but she could be jolly too. I remember one time she stuck some licorice in her mouth and gave me a big smile looking like she didn't have no front teeth and the floor walker caught her at it. We laughed and laughed about that. And Roselle Schimmelbeck who had an apartment down the hall from me at the assisted living center. She was all crippled up with arthritis but I never seen her anything but cheery. I used to go along to help her out at the grocery store and the last time we was there she was squeezing the Twinkies to make sure they was fresh and the filling came shooting out the end of the wrapper like toothpaste out of a tube. The two of us got to giggling so much we couldn't hardly get through the check-out line.

73

Yep. I'm gonna be writing down names on a piece of paper and pin it to my night dress so as to have it handy when I die 'cause what I want to be doing when I get across that bridge is laughing with friends and dancing with Fred Astaire.

Knockers Up
Donna Halvorson

The thing about winter is that it allows time for reflection.

For some reason or another, my thoughts turned to 1959. That was the year the Russians landed on the moon.

We watched it on a 13 inch black and white TV. The picture was so snowy we could hardly see it. But it was history.

Minnesota beat Iowa that year for a bid to the Rose Bowl. They lost.

John F. Kennedy ran for president, the first Catholic to do so. He won.

Female comics were rare in those days but I remember Rusty Warren. She was hilarious but considered a bit naughty. By today's standards she wouldn't even be a blip on the radar.

Then my thoughts turned to age 16. I was fully grown with a nice figure except for one thing. I was flat-chested. I would look longingly at the voluptuous beauties on the silver screen and then look in the mirror and see nothing, my bra size was 32 nothing. My boobs looked like two fried eggs. I would compensate by wearing scarves and ruffled blouses and a push-up bra to cover the void. I was very self-conscious. It didn't help that my two older sisters were well-endowed.

After suffering through the teen years I got on with my life and married my husband (I guess he married me for my mind).

When the babies came I suddenly had boobs. Of course they leaked a bit but I didn't mind. They filled out my clothes and when the milk dried up so did the boobs.

One day I was looking through a catalog and lo and behold there was the solution. It was a bra with pockets and fake rubber boobs, three sizes. I chose the smallest. For years I walked around with my head up and my chest out.

Then middle age set in and with it a few pounds here and there. I finally had some boobs. Of course it also meant a bigger backside and a larger tummy. At least the proportion was better.

Well here I am way past middle age and things have changed again.

Gravity has done its job. My push-up bra has been replaced with a pull-up bra. The result looks like a sack of mush. The word sexy is no longer part of my vocabulary. That's okay because most of my friends can't see so they can't tell the difference and those that can see can't remember.

But I remember the famous words of Rusty Warren.

"Knockers up, girls!"

"My Boy Lollipop"
(and other Golden Oldie Musical Offenses.)
Benj Mahle

Recently a news sources revealed the emergence of an I-phone application—an "app," to we who are witless in digital age computerspeak—that lets the user watch other people play video games. Not an app to play games, but to watch others play games: that is the lure. Clearly, I thought, this is but one more bastard offspring of the Apple seed, another thread in the Illuminati tapestry to further promote an even more sedentary, socially isolated generation, vulnerable to the manipulation of global puppeteers. A few hours later, having spent our gambling allowance, my wife and I cruised the floor of the Danbury casino watching a mostly pre-baby boomer collection of shuffling geezers and blue-haired geezerettes stick twenty-dollar bills into the slick silvery mouths of slot machines. Ironically, these devices, with their colorful flashing lights and catchy jingles are reminiscent of the juke boxes of the 50's in which we willingly deposited quarters, often to hear the most inane lyrics ever put to tunes with a musical range of six notes or less.

Like the jukebox, slot machines can be played with small change. Novice gamblers are led to think a fortune can be won by betting a penny, but "penny machine" is a lure, and a cruel deception: the only people betting pennies are old men resigned otherwise to watching their old women bet 30 to 300 pennies at a time. She does so with an urgency and passion he hasn't seen since the 50's when he thanked whoever put the "bop in the bop shi bop shi bop," and the "ram in the ramma ramma ding dong," for making her fall in love with him. He was her "boy lollipop," she his "Venus in blue jeans," his "Mona Lisa with a ponytail". Now he has the ponytail and she long ago retired any hope of fitting into blue jeans.

It's not uncommon to see one of these players tapping at two machines, several hundred dollars in each one, and betting the max— usually at least 3 dollars.

Seems insane, eh? But slot machines are an ingenious compilation of features designed from studies of human behavior to engage a player and keep that player engaged no matter how quickly his or her money disappears. (ATM services are close at hand; no one need ever go broke.) Each machine, which runs about 25K, sports color and form to lure anyone who has ever had a romantic or heroic notion. The screens are peopled with busty, long-legged women, swarthy, muscled young men, puppies, kittens, lusty guns and lilies, emperors, queens, black knights on white horses—something for everyone from rednecks to poets to redneck poets.

As we watch others play, we absorb the wails of delight equally with the groans of near misses, knowing that the wails generate great revenue for the casino, as it is the rare big win that keeps people playing, and usually reinvesting their winnings—plus some—in that same visit. There is an 800 number, posted above the exit doors, which offers help, "When gambling becomes more than a game." For most players it's a final insult stacked upon the frustration of leaving with an empty wallet. "I just wanted to win enough to play awhile," is a common refrain. "Just enough to play!"

The worst day to visit the Danbury casino is Monday. With a free player's card, a person is given a chance at winning 5 to 50 dollars in player credit. It is called "nifty-fifty" day, I guess because of the chance at the fifty dollars and the chance that everyone at the casino this day will be at least 50. The awful price of Nifty-Fifty day is the music—an endless playing and replaying of the tunes we somehow were compelled to lay out jukebox quarters to hear back in the day.

On the positive side, the casino offers great food at a low price: a prime rib sandwich that feeds two of us, for 5.99, as an example. Free soda or coffee. Clean accommodations and pleasant servers. It's a nice place, and pretty well ventilated. And we are not forced to succumb to the lure of free casino money. We would not have to endure the music had we stayed home, or driven to Duluth. But what were we ever thinking, feeling, dreaming, drinking or smoking that we made hits of "Puppy Love," "Venus in Blue Jeans," "The Flying Purple People-eaters," "It's My Party (and I'll cry if I want to)" and worst of all those horrible weepers on the Romeo and Juliet theme, like "Teen Angel," Girl is killed retrieving his class ring from their car stalled on a railroad track. "Tell Laura I love her," boy dies in stock car race trying to earn money for Laura's ring. "Running Bear," loves little White Dove but their tribes are enemies, so they drown together in a final, compromising embrace, and the lugubrious "Patches" my darling, from old Shanty Town – not darling enough, though, that the distraught adolescent would "grow a set" and stand up to the parent who opposes the relationship. Result? Girl feels unloved, drowns herself in a muddy river. (A win for the gene pool all around.)

The appeal of these songs is not heightened by the fact that all the males involved are either spineless wimps, poor drivers or weak swimmers. So why am I replaying them again here? Because seniors need to voice a protest; we can't just stand silently. For it's not just Mondays at a casino. Everywhere seniors gather there is an avalanche of 50's memorabilia that attack our senses. Sure, we loved the old cars, the corny westerns; we loved remembering soda fountains serving suicide Cokes; we loved thinking of ourselves as sweet and innocent with just a dash of naughty. But car lots don't sell Edsels, Hudsons, Packards, Studebakers. Theaters don't show westerns. People under 50 don't know a soda fountain from a fountain pen. Hell, they don't know what a fountain pen is. And while fifties music may have been a reflection of the moods, the angst, the joys, the prom and Homecoming themes of white teenagers then, why now must this be the one musical staple at any location where seniors gather: restaurants, big box stores, pharmacies…. casinos?

We've misplaced the yearbooks with the corsage pressed between the pages. Your letter jacket was donated to the Goodwill when you went off to the service—along with your baseball cards. Your Venus in blue jeans is more a Moms Mably in a smock. Still the tunes rain on us like teen angel's tears. Relax, my wife says: these were sweet songs, songs of innocence, romance, fun.

Thankfully, we long ago lost our innocence. The Kennedy assassination, Martin Luther King, James Meredith, the Vietnam War. These events introduced a new set of dismal lyrics. But at least there was no more "Mona Lisa with a ponytail," or conjurings of the goddess Venus for help in the love hunt. I.e., "Venus if you will….please send to me a girl for me to thrill. A girl who wants my kisses and my arms, a girl with all the charms, (But hopefully NOT the arms) of you.

Stupidly, sadly, drone-like, we tolerate the ubiquitous Nifty Fifty music for the sake of 5 to 50 dollars free play. My bride says the songs are sweet and fun; innocent, honest. I'm glad she's less cynical. But really: My Boy Lollipop? "You make my heart go …Giddy up. You set my soul on fi er. You are my one de si er." Just what is it you do with a lollipop, Sucker?

Swim Class
Craig Falkum

I learned to swim out of necessity. In 7th grade gym class, the boys had to file into the pool room one day each week for swimming. We were to learn all of the basic strokes plus some rudimentary dives.

The instructor lined us up according to our self-proclaimed ability to swim. I confessed that I couldn't swim and was sent to sit on the edge of the pool in the shallow end. We all took our respective places—good swimmers on the 9' deep end, non-swimmers on the 3' shallow end and fair swimmers in between. And we were naked.

Yes, naked as jaybirds. It was some sort of a health rule, but the girls got to wear tank suits when they used the pool on alternate days. Nobody could explain that. After a while we boys got used to each other, probably because we saw each other naked in the gym showers. Some boys had a mound of pubic hair, most had a few strands and a wimpy kid named Blair Wiemer had none. He was quickly nicknamed Bare Wiener.

The pool room had a door on each end. The boys came out of the door by the diving board and the girls came out the door on the shallow end. The girls' door was always locked when we swam and vice versa. One day we had a general free period. As I was sitting, naked, on the shallow end edge, I heard whispering. I looked around and saw that there was a small space under the girls' door and I could see the bottom ½ inch of several bare feet. GIRLS' bare feet! To my horror, my gaze surveyed a keyhole! Holy cow! The girls are looking at us through the keyhole! I leaped into the shallow end and put my head underwater to hide. And I didn't drown! Maybe I can swim! I began thrashing about with my arms and kicking my feet and I actually propelled myself across the pool without touching my feet on the bottom. I turned around and did it again. Then I pulled myself along the side of the pool to the ladder on the deep end (away from prying eyes) and climbed out.

"Mr. Stewart, I can swim!"

"Okay, we'll test you next week," he replied. The bell rang and I happily headed for the sanctity of the showers.

The next week I was feeling confident. I had already seen what happens when you dive in and can't swim. One of the kids jumped in the deep end and sank like a stone to the bottom. Mr. Stewart had a long aluminum pole and was poking him with it hoping he'd grab it, but the kid didn't, so Mr. Stewart dove into the pool without even taking off his t-shirt (he wore swim trunks) and brought the kid up to the surface. The kid coughed a bit, but was okay and was sent to the shallow end. I had never seen a grownup move so fast and act so decisively. I guessed kids nearly drowned all the time and Mr. Stewart had to jump in to save them on a regular basis, so I had no fear that Mr. Stewart would save me if I got into trouble.

Only I didn't get into trouble. I stood on the deep end hoping that I was just a blur as seen through the girls' keyhole, but if I failed I would be seen as clear as a bell in all my shriveled glory, as I sat on the shallow end of the pool. So I dove in, head under water, feet kicking, arms stroking as I easily made the other side of the pool. I swam back again.

"Well done," said Mr. Stewart, "take a spot about halfway down the pool." *Halfway?* Well, I could hide behind a lot more boys at the halfway point, so I was satisfied.

One day the girls were mistakenly let into the pool room when we boys were swimming. We were all sitting on the edge of the pool and Clifford Young was on the board about to demonstrate a dive. Just then, we heard a creak from the shallow end and watched as the girls started to stream into the pool room in their tank suits--one piece loose fitting blue swim suits that didn't give anyone a thrill. The first ones took a few steps in and stopped and stared at us as the ones behind began to push and shove and wonder why they stopped. Then they began to push and shove more vigorously as they *did* realize why the first ones stopped. We boys let out a shriek and jumped into the pool in unison. Except for Clifford Young. He was like a deer in headlights as he stood there, buck naked, facing the girls' door.

"What do I do?" he said.

"Jump, Clifford, jump!" we screamed, but it took an eternity before he actually did jump. Soon Miss Christianson, the shapely, young, blond gym instructor, forced her way into the pool room and herded her girls back behind their door and shut and locked it.

We got to swim with the girls only once in the three years I attended Bryant Junior High and that was at the end of our 9th grade year. The girls didn't wear their school tank suits but had their own swimsuits, even some two-piece suits.

For some strange reason, being in the pool with the girls was exciting. Nearly all of the boys had erections poking through their swimsuits. So, naturally our instructor had the boys come up and demonstrate certain dives. We boys would walk up half bent over to try to conceal our condition and dive in as fast as we could while the girls gawked and tittered and smirked. Mr. Allen was our instructor that year. He was chuckling all the time while we did twisted gyrations and bent over poses to try to hide our excitement. Miss Christianson was also there. She was the Nordic bombshell gym teacher that strode through the halls in her white gym shorts, causing the male teachers to leer out the glass classroom doors while the more matronly women teachers huffed sighs of disgust. During our one co-ed swim, somebody pushed Miss Christianson into the pool and she emerged with her white gym shorts and white blouse, now *translucent*. Clifford Young pulled me behind the diving board, Watch her when she dives off the board, he said, because she spreads her legs and you can see everything.

I wasn't even sure what everything was, but I'm still grateful to Clifford for that opportunity and to the swim class of Bryant Junior High for teaching me to swim and a whole lot more.

Small Memory
Peter Allen

I was an egg in a furry nest with cookie dough privileges. An active child, quick to anger and easily frightened, I was learning about the world beyond my Mother's lap, a devotee of *Wind in the Willows.*

My Father was a tall man, skinny and turning grey. He had an important job in the City writing for *Newsweek* about higher education. I thought he wrote about the older, taller kids in school but really he reported on Land Grant Colleges which were ceded land by the federal government for the purpose of agricultural education.

My Mother wanted tea and some "blink time." So my Dad and I took the boat I'd gotten for my fifth birthday down a big hill to the tidal pool on Long Island Sound. Across the water, Connecticut was barely visible on a clear day.

There were radio controlled boats big as my bike, sails fluttering in the unsteady breeze. A model plane was landing on the water and then taking off, noisier than our lawnmower and smelling worse than the mercurochrome Mom put on my skinned knees.

There were lots of big men with hairy arms wearing athletic tee shirts. Ignorant that not everyone was kind, I was surprised that one of the men got angry when our unguided boat collided with his fancy one.

We were dowsing for a nice day. My Father set the sails on our little boat and pushed it off shore. A light wind carried our boat faster than the others and we collected our craft from the opposite shore over and over. It was a fine afternoon and we were sailors.

Onkel Julius

(a true story of Julius Sommerfeld)

Marcia Savela

In the year 1901 Wilhelm II, grandson of Queen Victoria and cousin to Tsar Nicholas of Russia, was the Kaiser (Emperor) of Germany. Germany at this time was in an alliance game and posturing for respect as they were losing diplomatic relationships, thus setting the stage for WW I.

November first of that year my Onkel (Uncle) Julius was born. He is the youngest of eight Sommerfeld children. Emily, my Grossmutter (Grandmother), was the eldest followed by Emil, Olga, Johanna, Lotta, Ottilia and August.

Under Hitler the New Germany was being built. Onkel Julius worked in construction. He spent long hours of continuous usage of the jack hammer. By the time he was in his early 30's, he was confined to a wheelchair because of damage to his muscles and nerves. Fortunately Julius was married to the loving Paula, who was devoted to him. Tante (Aunt) Paula deeply loved the man she called, "Mein Liebe Suss" (My Sweet Love).

Tante Paula's friend was the proprietor of the local grocery and begged Paula to greet her with the mandatory German Greeting of Heil Hitler. If Paula continued to refuse, both of them could be reported. Everyone cringed with fear of the informers.

Children at the age of seven attended Hitler Camps to be indoctrinated with the Gospel of the Fuhrer. The Third Reich was not a political party but a cult that used religious symbols to attract people. It was these Hitler Camp Youths who were the frequent informers.

To comply, Tante made a fist with her left hand and put it in her pocket. With the right hand the mandatory greeting. Under her breath she would say, "Schwein Schwartz". Her greeting was, "Heil Hitler you black pig". This made the greeting palatable for my aunt. A small but poignant act of courage.

In January 1934, the Reich created a new law to correct a genetic flaw in some Germans--by forced sterilization. Over 400,000 Germans were cleansed. Also, the Reich would care for those who were mentally or physically impaired, no matter how slight the defect, they would be sent to grand houses in the country where they would be cared for and be safe.

As the allied bombs reached Germany, bomb shelters were created. My aunt was approached to consider having Julius sent to one of those wonderful Reich facilities. She refused.

The town Burgermeister (Mayor) was a family friend and had informed Paula that these wonderful facilities, once filled, were bombed. Reported to be by allied bombs, but in reality it was by German bombs, the Luftwaffe (air weapon). Germans annihilating Germans--just another correction of a flaw by the Third Reich.

Paula was approached a second time, again she refused. This time, she was informed that Julius would have to wait outside the shelter until the entire able-bodied town folk were inside. If there was enough room, then and only then, could Julius and his wheel chair enter. Paula always waited outside next to Julius and the town folk always found room for Julius and his chair.

In 1945, Hitler was the Fuhrer (driver) only until April 30th. The Hamburg radio announced that Hitler died in battle. On December 30th, Hitler's will was found confirming his intentions to commit suicide. December 1st of that year, the Nurenbrug trials began for 24 Nazi war criminals. Appropriately it was conducted in the Nurenburg Palace of Justice. December 1st also marked the passing of my Onkel Julius. He was only 44 years of age. He had however, survived WW I, WW II and Hitler.

I do not know what my Onkel Julius looked like. I only have a photo of his grave site. But through Tante Paula telling me his story, I did get to know of him, and now so do you.

Father's Day
Nancy Hengeveld

This is for all you who lost your father at a young age. Or you did have a father, but he was suffering from post-traumatic stress disorder after fighting in a war, or from alcohol or drug addiction, or from some other type of mental illness, and he couldn't be there for you. Or he existed but was emotionally or physically absent for whatever reason. Or he was abusive to family members, and you wish he would have left. Or he disappeared, and you never heard from him again. Or he promised to visit you as much as possible, but rarely showed up. Or maybe you never even knew who he was. Or he never knew you.

This is for you who found yourselves breaking a multigenerational cycle of fatherless fathers. Somehow, you found a way to redeem the next generation in your family. It wasn't easy. You know who you are. This is especially for you.

This is for all you fathers and stepfathers who got up in the morning, got your children off to school, helped them with their homework, took care of them when they were sick, played ball with them, read to them and taught them the important things of life even though you didn't have a dad to do that with you when you were a kid.

You're lucky, because you're the resilient ones. You survived a childhood without a father to become nurturing fathers yourselves. Sociologists believe that one of the factors of resiliency is having another father figure in your life—a teacher, coach, relative, neighbor or an adult friend who was a role model for you.

So this is for you men who mentor and nurture children and teens in your work, in your neighborhoods, in your faith communities, in your volunteer work and in your extended families and friendships. You may be more important to some child than you'll ever know, even though you may not be fathers yourselves.

Psychologist and developmental theorist Erik Erickson called the task of nurturing the next generation "generativity" and considered it the most important task of middle adulthood. He called the failure to nurture the next generation "stagnation." (Think of a stagnant pond and its inability to sustain new life.) Stagnation is described as self-absorption and self-preoccupation with one's own needs.

To all of you fathers and father figures who may never have a building or a street or a statue in a park named after you but are living quiet lives of caring and are successfully completing the task of "generativity," know that your influence will live long beyond your own life in future generations of parents.

Booker T. Washington said, "Success is to be measured not so much by the position that one has reached in life as by the obstacles which he has overcome while trying to succeed." Not having a father is a huge obstacle you've overcome.

Okay, so you're not perfect. You don't have to be. What you're doing is enough.

The Bride's Tail
Nicholas Ozment

Quimby the woodcutter met his mysterious bride one afternoon in early spring, just as he was about to put his axe to the bole of a tall, black poplar. The tree grew alone in a glade near a creek.

A woman's voice stopped him.

"Not that tree."

She had slipped like a faun into the glade.

He checked his swing and lowered the axe-head to the ground. Leaning on the long handle, he admired the visitor.

She wore a green jerkin that covered little. She was short and athletically built. Tawny freckles were sprinkled liberally over her smooth skin. Her long hair was the color of flame, a deeper red than his own.

"Why shan't I cut down this tree?"

"That is a gateway tree." She shrugged, one corner of her lip curling in a half-smile, as if she were having to explain something very elementary to a silly young boy. "If you fell it, it will draw you through, never to return."

He raised a bushy eyebrow. "Draw me through to where?"

"Wild Wood. The shadow wood of the Fey. You are mortal. You could not come back."

He contemplated this, stroking his thick beard. "Well, there aren't too many who would miss me. My parents are buried, and I have never taken a mate. Is there good mead in the Wild Wood?"

She smiled. "There are draughts there the likes of which man has never tasted."

"Is that good or bad?"

"Can you imagine drinking the first warm rays of a spring morning?" She drew nearer to him, lithe and graceful as a stalking cat.

"Or the first chill of an autumn evening, right before you climb beneath warm blankets with a lover?"

He huffed. "I reckon I'd already have to be well into my cups to imagine any of that. Are you a bard? You like your metaphor more than I like my mead."

"My name," she said with a slight smirk that made his heart ache in an altogether new way, "is Embla."

Quimby could not have guessed he would be talking to another living soul when he arose that morning, much less flirting with this strange otherworldly beauty. Yet he laid his axe aside, and began to walk with her, and he soon found himself sitting beside her on the grassy bank of the creek. They talked and teased and laughed, and he stole glances into her hazel eyes, and it began to feel to him – although he certainly had no prior experience with which to compare it – something like courtship.

Before he knew it, dusk was upon them. She arose from the bank and slinked away into the growing shadows of the forest as silently as she had come. He, too, arose and – after first locating his axe where he had absent-mindedly leaned it against a tree stump -- returned alone to his cottage.

The next day he went back to the glade, and after a while she again appeared. Thereafter he visited her often, and by the time summer was in full heat he was passionately in love. In the autumn of that same year, he took her before the village priest.

But he had never told anyone from whence she had come, and on the day of the wedding there were many villagers leery of the whole affair. They were suspicious of her accent, and there were grumblings that she came from the North, an abandoned Viking wench. Some whispered that she was a witch. And there was one who hinted that she was not human at all.

It was an outdoor wedding on a crisp sunny day. Leaves splashed in autumn's colors provided the festivity's only decoration.

When the priest asked if there were any present who might object to the union, three men stepped forth. Their leader was a hunter named Bernard, who revealed that he had spied on Embla and discovered her secret: she was indeed from the North, but she was no Saxon. She was a hulder, a young female troll. "I...have seen her tail."

Embla blushed, while her husband-to-be flushed red with anger.

Bernard and his two lackeys brazenly tromped toward Embla, across the crackling leaves that carpeted the processional aisle, intent on proving their bold claim. A few other men from the village, emboldened, fell in behind them.

Embla, her wet hazel eyes flashing, darted into the woods. Quimby fought three of the villagers off with his bare hands, but others, wanting to see with their own eyes if it be true, took up the chase and followed Embla. She was nimble and clever, but Bernard was accustomed to tracking prey, and she could not shake the small band of men he led.

She ran, weaving up rocky paths and down into deep defiles, ignoring scrape of thorn and thistle as she tried to shake her pursuers. Her wedding dress in tatters, she crouched by the creek where she and Quimby had first talked, cupping a few quick drinks to her lips. She leapt up when she once again heard her pursuers calling her name and sprinted deeper into the woods.

She scrambled to the crest of a hill and froze. A hulking silhouette stood beneath a yew tree.

"Qu-Quimby?"

He stepped into the light of the setting sun, his axe balanced on one broad shoulder.

A mixture of uncertainty and fear flashed across her features that had so recently conveyed perfect admiration and love. "What, Quimby, do you intend to do with that axe?"

He grunted and strode toward her. She stood her ground.

Her head was level with the red chest hairs that curled out between the leather straps of his tunic.

She lifted her gaze to his gray eyes. "Are you going to chop off my tail? ... Or my head?"

His free arm reached out, and he clasped her small fingers in his own calloused hand. "I've become rather fond of both. Come this way."

As they scrambled through the deep woods, their destination soon became clear: he was taking her back to the place where they first met.

When they reached the glade, Quimby let go her hand and took the axe from his shoulder, hoisting it in his firm grip.

She gasped as he hefted the axe. "You must not—I have told you what will happen!"

He grunted. "Let them follow us into the Wild Wood."

Her fingers wrapped around his bulging arm, ineffectually tugging him back. "You will never be able to return!"

He shook her off. "We'll lift a cup to our nuptials in the Wild Wood! I'm eager to know what it tastes like to drink the first chill of winter, the first rays of spring."

The pursuers heard the sound of chopping afar off. But when they reached the glade, all they found was a felled black poplar. Two sets of tracks—large boot soles and dainty bare feet—were seen all around the stump, but no trail could be found leaving the glade. Quimby and his bride were never seen again.

Footnote to Doggerel
Tom Driscoll

"Poetry is not for the faint of heart." /[i]

April gruel. The steady locomotion of shoveling. Smith O'Connor pried up a heavy seven-inch slice of pure white snow, his mother a Polaroid fading from memory: blue plates of moist angel cake in each hand, a piece for him and one for his dad, father and son having, long-agone, just cleared and spread coal cinders on icy sidewalks. When he might have just as well longed for the past, Smith chuckled at the irony. His father, dead of a heart attack shoveling snow, lay frozen for thirty winters. His mother, herself already five winters iced, fell victim to rotten wires and loose screws.

All night long, from the great deafness of distant, half dead townships, had snowplows grumbled down One-Ten, exploding on the half hour past Gap Tooth and Smith's towering house of forty-nine windows swaddled in blue spruce against the bluff. All night long, the thundering hush of oversized flakes blanketing his long, steep driveway tossed him, turned him, deranging his thoughts into a frosty epicpoem sluiced through with a remotely haunting chorus.

> The woods are lovely, dark and deep,
> But I have promises to keep … /[ii]

Around 5 a.m., Smith's wife Frances slipped back into bed after a trip to the bathroom. A few heartbeats later, short of breath and exhausted, escaped the old poet into a subconscious warren / finds himself in a nanosecond illuminated by the cryptic torch of Dream / what's been hounding him / the wintery months passed since his beloved friend Jakes died in a freakish creek side collision involving young Shadow and a panicked buck with an arrow stuck through its neck.

The wide, ice white riverscape's blinding / when the woman's plaintive grunt / pop, pop, pop. Her broom straw hair splays out from under her bulky camo cap meant to cover little, dried apricot ears. A smirk of terminal clumsiness dimpling her ruddy cheeks, is she shortly and in slowed motion all abumble upon the broken surface of thin ice. Frozen momentarily above frigid black water murkied all the muddier under two feet of regurgitated snowmobile slush, her insulated, duck colored coveralls wick certain death as she grapples futilely / gravity / for breath befuddled.

As Dream cam claws for a wide shot of porcelain dog / ice chunks yaw inside jagged ice ring where down clad in soggy brown numb, woman has just knifed through / bitterly heaves back the breathlessly cold drink she flogs / pitches albino dog himself into Dream's black deeps.

Massive paws maul the still about the hole. His powerful jaws snap bergs into powder / icicles fanged & snags sugar crusted cuff of dunked woman's durable canvas sleeve. Summoning strength few save said snow colored Dream dog could possibly possess, pulls out the beast drencht drowning woman from the hypothermic slackwaterpool / tows he her hull across skyblue to rusty Dreamer's pickup frozen truck inside ice block aqua sinks / has he / she / is saved / was lost.

Steam as off a stewpot lid hugs her / she slues a quavering arm over Dream dog's sturdy platinum pelt / buries her pearled face in a bush of warm hide swaddling the beast's droopy ears / inhales the unwashed smell of dog brush & bedding / he as always nonchalantly heroic & hungry.

Her lips are thin and stiff and black like his, only terser, the worse, hers, for the fleeting terror of freezing stiff. Granite halos encrust her grateful winter twilight colored eyes. His are ceramic bowls of wild red honey. Doggoboy detects egg whites and wheat toast in the gaps of the woman's smoke stained teeth and steals a lick off, he / her paled steel face laps / her / he pelf.

The woman rubs his black nose with hers-o-rosy / purrs, "Goo boy," and tugs open a brass breast pocket whisper / produces a small glass phial and a silver spoon / zippers: "Here you go, goo boy," pouring sticky lacquer the color of liquid sapphires, "Lil this'll make you feel real / bring me's back / soon's you awakes / s'spoon here."

Goo boy licks clean the / chomps down on the intricately tooled stemware's silver saucer / bolts onto the ice and vanishes, thought-like / clencht fangs clutcht / poof / wakes up dreamt of / poet did? Dog-gone? Verses?

Smith slid his ergonomic orange snow shovel under another half

96

foot of fresh white sod. O, cruel, damn you, April, O. Acting on him like a narcotic, reality distended, the truth left maladroit, the noble Dream remembered felt irresponsible. And that made him feel guilty. He should have known / never in the first place been / better than / on the ice to be below the lock & dam at Dresbach.

Smith's brain chopped sloppy Dream ice, scraping image after image off the pavement, sorting through Facts even as Facts turned fluid. He caught a glimpse of his reflection in a large, vaguely warped window / young and but yet old man hunched over a bent spoon scooping sniffles from a drainage swale.

Smith dropped his head, shoved wet snow thirty feet across to the neighbor's picket fence, hoisted soup onto a slushy mound, melted down from eight feet to four feet high during a cynical warm snap back in early March. The Dream / poem itself / near dissipated, Smith no longer felt good that his black Border Collie Shadow had goosed open & leapt through the sliding back window / saved from drowning that DNR officer, an unselfish duck woman who simply tried to stop him-Smith from driving out on ice no longer safe even for fishing. He just felt guilty, guilty and stupid; stupid for sacrificing the pickup, which wouldn't be salvaged off the river bottom until barge season; guilty for leaving his white retriever Jakes lying on the front seat wrapped in the threadbare blue dog bone blanket he'd slept with most of his life, already twelve hours dead when ice started to buckle beneath the truck in a bungled attempt at a sea burial that, in bleak retrospect, struck Smith silly as a way to honor a beloved pet, albeit a water-loving pet, selfish, impetuous, immature as any puppy love ever / up bolts old poemsmith / Frances, beside herself-half-asleep-worried-sick about Smith, stirs and murmurs, "Wass bride lied?" Silvered spoon is a tongue of flame / igneous in black Shadow's snowy maw clamped / champs hero hard down on darkness. Smith momentarily caresses Frances' warm fingers, like a poem a soft dog ear / tries to say, "Good night, my love," how every night he does, but instead says "Goo bye, my Wolf,"/ ⁱⁱⁱ / when Smith his chest has clutcht, and as loudly can only grouse, "Promises, I kept!" just as the tumult of snowplows tumbled past.

ⁱ *I Remain, The Letters of Lew Welch, Vol Two*, (Grey Fox Press, 1980). Letter fragment, Welch to Elspeth Smith, June 1969. Welch vanished without a trace

97

in 1970.

[ii] "Stopping by a Woods on A Snowy Evening", <u>New Hampshire</u>, Robert Frost, (Holt, 1923). In December 1962, Frost suffered a severe heart attack and died in January 1963.

[iii] <u>*Doggerel, Posthumous Collected Love Poems*</u>, Smith O'Connor, edited by Dr. O. Frances Margarita, (Trumpet Tear Editions, 2020). Author of many books, he is best known for retelling the Orpheus & Eurydice myth in <u>Pearl</u>, an account of his missionary daughter's abduction by a rebel warlord in Eastern Congo. Pearl's eventual rescue during the January 2002 eruption of Nyirangongo volcano near Goma was facilitated by Kadogo, a dog she raised and trained herself. O'Connor trained Army combat dogs in Georgia during the Vietnam War. He died long ago when his heart gave out on a cruel April morning.

Review of *Chronology* by Peter Allen
Nicole Borg

Peter Allen's collection of poetry, *Chronology*, follows the poet's story where the line between truth and imagination is blurred. Within Allen's narrative is a memorable cast of characters, which he brings to life through dialogue and precise description. There's Brooks from the store who tells the speaker "dairy products were all poison,/that cloven hoofs were unclean/that only urine and cashews could purify" or Charles who was "an easy talker/friendly as a cat in a dairy barn" but who "could not forgive himself for abandoning his children". With few words, Allen tells us much. But the most vivid character of all is the speaker.

Allen tells the story of the speaker with a directness that leaves the reader wanting one more poem, one more story to better understand his life chronology. As a child the speaker "did my due diligence,/ packed the car like a Beverly/Hillbilly, the back seat full/of heavy things, the floor rusting/through. She was drinking/and driving when I was counting/phone poles just over the county line." In every poem is a humility, a humor at the strange events of life, a want for peace. "When I see clearly, /my heart sings like a bird/noting the time of day,/calling out, 'We're here!/We're here!'"

The theme of peace is strong as Allen reveals a reverence for nature, dogs and cats, children, women, all living things. The language he uses elevates these subjects to an almost spiritual state. "Today gave the gift of a flat stone and Dwarf/Trout Lilies growing here and only here." and later he says, "Spread my ashes here so I may return again." When speaking to young men he advises "Build a birdhouse./Hang it up./Find out the right way./Walk a dirt road/barefoot./Tell your Mom she's pretty./Make a plan/then do it/Repeat./When you find love,/stay." Allen creates a very real character in the speaker, grounded in nature and love.

Chronology is a lovely collection of poetry that causes the reader to consider the world in a new way. Allen's directness and clear description has a celebratory quality that illustrate the bad in life but encourage the reader to dwell rather on what is good and to appreciate life's innumerable gifts even amidst that which is difficult. Allen's work is full of beauty and humor and keen observation and makes for an enjoyable read.

Contributors Notes

Peter Allen is a 62 year old resident of Faribault. He took up writing as a serious hobby about five years ago. He doesn't know where his poems come from. Inspiration is a fickle mistress. He carries a small notebook so that he can note any odd or interesting thoughts that come to him. Then he tries to make sense of his ideas. He wishes for all of us that we have more than one muse.

Patricia Barone, in addition to *The Scent of Water*, a collection of poetry recently out from Blue Light Press in San Francisco, has published a novella, *The Wind*, and a book of poetry, *Handmade Paper*, with New Rivers Press. Her poetry has been anthologized by numerous publishers, including New Rivers Press and Prentice Hall. She has also published short stories. Her awards include a Loft-McKnight Award of Distinction in poetry, a Lake Superior Contemporary Writers Award for a short story, and a Minnesota State Arts Board Career Opportunity Grant for a workshop with the Irish poet Eavan Boland.

Peg Bauernfeind hopes someday to be recognized as a Minnesota writer. She lives in Wabasha on a backwater of the Mississippi River with her dog Woody. Her real writing career started when she retired and wrote the Danny Malloy series about a teenaged boy exploring the river. *A Vision Takes Flight* is her latest adventure, written with C.J. Halvorson for the National Eagle Center in Wabasha. Peg enjoys being part of the Rural America Writers' Center.

Betty J. Benner is a poet/essayist who has lived in southeast Minnesota all of her life, since 1950 in Austin. She seeks to convey who she is in her writing and strives to connect present, past, and future. She has been published locally—*Green Blade* magazine, various newspapers, Crossings at Carnegie. Enjoyed hugely her visits to the Rural America Writers' Center in Plainview. Published and edited two versions of the *Millpond Journal*, 1997 and 1998. Currently belongs to a local writers group. Wrote her first poem in first grade:

> "Red
> Sled."

Dee Bezoier Minnesota Native. Small towns, then Edina HS & UM. Varied work until retired. Plainview open-mic for several years of reading ultra-condensed essays (pieces) he might also term "poexpressays" – or not. No matter: readers and listeners make up their own minds. (Welcome aboard!)

Nicole Borg is a full-time mom, former English teacher and school librarian, and co-editor of the *Green Blade*. Her poetry and prose have appeared in various publications throughout MN. In 2014, she received an Emerging Artists grant from the Southeastern Minnesota Arts Council to complete her first poetry manuscript *All Roads Lead Home*. She lives in Wabasha on the lovely Mississippi with her husband and two sons.

Tim J. Brennan, an educator for over thirty years, writes from Austin, MN. His poetry can be found in many nice places including the *Green Blade*, *Talking Stick*, KAXE public radio, *The Lake* (U.K.) and many others. Brennan's one act plays have been produced on many nice stages including White Bear Lake MN, Chicago, San Diego, Rochester MN, and Bethesda MD.

Dan Butterfass is a poet and outdoorsman living in Rochester, Minnesota with his family. His work has been published in journals such as *Cave Wall*, *The Café Review*, and *Great River Review*.

Emilio DeGrazia has several small press books published, and will have a collection of personal essays, *Chirps: Making Small Waves*, published by Shipwreckt Books in the fall, 2015. He is a past Poet Laureate of Winona, Minnesota, where he lives with his wife Monica.

Tom Driscoll is the author of *Ondine & the Blue Troll* (Rocket Science Press 2012). His work has appeared in many small magazines and newspapers over the years, including *Me Too, the Raven* and *The Mississippi Valley Review*. He is the managing editor of *Lost Lake Folk Opera* magazine, and lives in Rushford, Minnesota.

P.S. (Penny) Duffy lives in Rochester, MN. Since 2001 she has published poetry, flash fiction, creative nonfiction, and essays and is the author of three books, including *A Stockbridge Homecoming* (Bright Sky Press, 2001), a memoir of her family's time in 1940s China where she was born. Her debut novel *The Cartographer of No Man's Land* (W. W. Norton, 2013) takes place during the First World War and was a Barnes and Noble Discover pick, highlighted by Oprah magazine, and a finalist for the 2014 International Dayton Literary Peace Prize, which honors the power of literature to foster peace.

Craig Falkum is a retired civil engineer who was born and raised in Minneapolis and now lives in Wabasha, Minnesota with his wife, Nancy. Together they owned and operated an independent bookstore for 14 years before economics won out. He has had previous work published in *Green Blade* and *The Talking Stick*. He enjoys bicycling and attempting home repairs.

Kate Halverson is the author of six books, *EveryWoman's Journey* most recently available via Amazon/Barnes & Noble. She is presently looking for both an agent/publisher for a family memoir entitled *Reaching Up to Touch Bottom*. A **BOOK ART** advocate, Kate spends most of her free-time, either creating her own art, photographing road trips or reading about others — non-fiction, her favorite genre.

Donna Halvorson is a resident of Lake City, MN. A retired interior designer (30 yrs) and retired realtor (25 yrs), she was educated in Lake City schools, University of Minnesota and Kaplan University. Author of two books "Skip a Stone" and "When Life Throws Tomatoes Make Bloody Marys," her work has been featured in *Green Blade, Today Magazine, Rochester Post Bulletin* and *City Remembers*. After a lifetime of organizations. committee meetings and social causes, Donna enjoys retirement along the Mississippi and continues writing, reading, and socializing.

Nancy Hengeveld's poetry has been published in *Dust and Fire, Talking Stick*, and *Green Blade,* and she wrote a monthly column for the *Rochester Post Bulletin* for 13 years. She is an active member of the Rural American Writers' Center in Plainview. She taught psychology at Rochester Community and Technical College and works as a licensed psychologist with a private practice in Rochester. She lives in Preston with her husband near the state bike trail.

Jennifer Jesseph has been writing for over thirty years. She loves writing in rhyme and writing for children and adults. She is currently working on performance poetry pieces for adults and getting serious about using puppets with children at school. She lives in Pine Island with her husband and college age children.

Melissa Lammers is a graduate of Winona State University with a BFA in studio art. Living in rural Minnesota with her family, she works from her home studio while raising two children. Her work ranges from pastel drawings to thrown ceramics.

Benj Mahle is a Plainview native and a 1963 graduate. After graduating from Winona State in 1972, he found the best job in the world, and taught English in Rochester for nearly 40 years. The author of two teaching manuals, he has also self-published a poetry collection and a book of prose sketches and essays with---hopefully--a novel or collection of short plays, to follow. (No more rejection notices for this guy!) Married since 1966, he has a son, daughter, grandson and twin dachshunds he treasures. He enjoys fishing, family, geezer softball, stories of love and vengeance, Arizona winters, and friends.

Ken McCullough is the current Poet Laureate of Winona, Minnesota. His most recent book of poetry (his eighth) is *Broken Gates*, from Red Dragonfly Press. He is working on a manuscript based on interviews he conducted with farmers on the ridge where he lives. McCullough is married to playwright Lynn Nankivil.

Susan McMillan learned to love poetry listening to her mother read nursery rhymes. This love was later fueled by an unforgettable English teacher, Violet Lorenson, to whom she owes her desire to write. She is inspired by nature and the work of other writers. Beyond participation in the Rural America Writers' Center, she leads Southeastern Minnesota Poets in Rochester and serves as a regional vice president for the League of Minnesota Poets.

Melissa McNallan is a columnist and reporter for the *Rochester Post Bulletin*. She enjoys writing poetry, short stories, and has been diligently working on a novel for a number of years.

Nicholas Ozment, who has an MA in English and is Chief Creative Officer of a Minnesota tour company, also offers his professional services as a ghostwriter, copy editor, and proofreader. He co-edited *MOOREEFFOC Magazine* and *Every Day Poets*, and has copy-edited published work ranging from horror by fiction authors to academic research by professors with PhDs. His own writing has appeared in over 100 publications. He enjoys exploring Minnesota back roads with his wife Melissa Lammers and their two children.

Kit Rohrbach lives, writes, and herds cats in Rochester, MN. Her latest book, *Typing Basics,* is a collection of poems and illustrations published by Zumbro River Press.

Marcia Savela has been writing poetry and short stories since high school, which reflect her heritage, family values and love of nature. Several of her works have been published. Her poetry reflects her Finnish heritage but her prose is generated by her German-Russian lineage. Blessings.

Su Smallen is the author of four collections of poetry. Honors for her work include nomination for the Pushcart Press Editors' Book Award for *Weight of Light* and Minnesota Book Award Finalist for *Buddha, Proof.* **www.susmallen.com**

Steven R. Vogel has been writing and performing music and poetry since age nine—churches, coffeehouses, schools, public gatherings, celebrations, contests, and poetry presentations (none more fun than Third Wednesdays!)—throughout four states. He has lived and worked on farms, in villages, and in cities of every size. He had attended seven grade schools by the time his family moved Up North. He is a graduate of Bemidji State University and of Mayo Medical School.

Rural America Writers' Center
Members 2015

Carolyn Bizien
Nicole Borg
Dan Butterfass
Emilio DeGrazia
Tom Driscoll
Penelope Duffy
Deirdre Flesche
Donna Halvorson
Dean Harrington
Sally Harrington
Rita Hawes
Nancy Hengeveld
Dag Knudsen
Benj Mahle
Susan McMillan
Nicholas Ozment
Marcia Savela
Gloria Smit
Steve Vogel

In addition to participating in activities sponsored by the RAWC, members support the Writers' Center with a $25 annual contribution. Members receive a free copy of the *Green Blade*, as well as a 10% discount on workshops and purchases made at *Commonsense Books*. Membership dues are good for one calendar year.

Interested in becoming a member? You can join at any Writers' Center event or mail a check, payable to RAWC, to the Rural America Writers' Center, 412 W. Broadway, Plainview, MN 55964